The Daily Greek Challenge

Learn 10 Greek Words a Day for 7 Weeks

Introduction

Welcome to "Learn 10 Greek Words a Day for 7 Weeks"! This book is designed to provide an engaging and effective learning experience for children and beginners who are eager to discover the beauty of the Greek language. With its carefully curated selection of words and interactive approach, this book aims to make language learning a fun and enjoyable journey.

Learning a new language can be both exciting and challenging, but fear not! We have crafted this book with your learning needs in mind. Each day, you will encounter a set of ten Greek words that are carefully chosen to be useful and practical in everyday situations. These words cover various themes, allowing you to expand your vocabulary and gain confidence in your language skills.

To facilitate your learning process, we have provided corresponding English words alongside the Greek words, allowing you to establish meaningful connections between the two languages. By actively engaging in writing down (4x) the correct Greek words, you will reinforce your memory and develop a solid foundation in the language. Embrace the joy of discovery as you unlock new words each day, steadily building your language skills one step at a time.

This book is meant to be your companion throughout the course of seven weeks, providing you with a structured learning experience. Each week is carefully planned to introduce new vocabulary while reinforcing previously learned words, allowing you to review and consolidate your knowledge. Make sure to allocate a few minutes each day to engage with the exercises and activities provided. Consistency is key, and your dedication will yield rewarding results.

Whether you are a young language enthusiast or a curious beginner, this book is designed to cater to your needs. The vibrant illustrations and interactive exercises are intended to spark your imagination and keep you engaged. Remember, learning a language should be an enjoyable experience, and we hope this book will ignite your passion for Greek.

As you embark on this language learning adventure, we encourage you to embrace the challenge, celebrate your progress, and have fun along the way. Learning 10 Greek words a day is an achievable goal, and with perseverance and dedication, you will unlock the doors to a new world of communication and understanding.

Happy learning!

Table of Contents

Week 1

Day 1: Numbers

One	Ένα
Two	Δύο
Three	Τρία
Four	Τέσσερα
Five	Πέντε
Six	Έξι
Seven	Επτά
Eight	Οκτώ
Nine	Εννέα
Ten	Δέκα

Write the right words down twice on the next page

Six	....	....
Two	....	....
Eight	....	....
Four	....	....
Five	....	....
Eight	....	....
Seven	....	....
Three	....	....
Nine	....	....
Ten	....	....
One	....	....
Two	....	....
Ten	....	....
Four	....	....
Five	....	....
Six	....	....
Seven	....	....
Three	....	....
Nine	....	....
One	....	....

Week 1

Day 2: Colors

Red	Κόκκινο
Blue	Μπλε
Yellow	Κίτρινο
Green	Πράσινο
Orange	Πορτοκαλί
Purple	Μωβ
Pink	Ροζ
Black	Μαύρο
White	Λευκό
Gray	Γκρι

Write the right words down twice on the next page

Red	....	....
Purple	....	....
White	....	....
Gray	....	....
Orange	....	....
Purple	....	....
Blue	....	....
Black	....	....
White	....	....
Gray	....	....
Pink	....	....
Blue	....	....
Yellow	....	....
Green	....	....
Orange	....	....
Pink	....	....
Red	....	....
Black	....	....
Yellow	....	....
Green	....	....

Week 1

Day 3: Family

Mother	Μητέρα
Father	Πατέρας
Brother	Αδελφός
Sister	Αδελφή
Son	Γιος
Daughter	Κόρη
Grandfather	Παππούς
Grandmother	Γιαγιά
Uncle	Θείος
Aunt	Θεία

Write the right words down twice on the next page

Aunt	....	....
Father	....	....
Mother	....	....
Uncle	....	....
Brother	....	....
Sister	....	....
Son	....	....
Daughter	....	....
Grandfather	....	....
Sister	....	....
Aunt	....	....
Grandmother	....	....
Uncle	....	....
Son	....	....
Grandmother	....	....
Father	....	....
Brother	....	....
Daughter	....	....
Grandfather	....	....
Mother	....	....

Week 1

Day 4: Food

Bread	Ψωμί
Rice	Ρύζι
Meat	Κρέας
Vegetables	Λαχανικά
Fruit	Φρούτα
Milk	Γάλα
Cheese	Τυρί
Eggs	Αυγά
Soup	Σούπα
Dessert	Επιδόρπιο

Write the right words down twice on the next page

Cheese	....	....
Meat	....	....
Dessert	....	....
Vegetables	....	....
Fruit	....	....
Milk	....	....
Vegetables	....	....
Eggs	....	....
Soup	....	....
Dessert	....	....
Bread	....	....
Rice	....	....
Meat	....	....
Fruit	....	....
Milk	....	....
Cheese	....	....
Bread	....	....
Eggs	....	....
Soup	....	....
Rice	....	....

Week 1

Day 5: Animals

Dog	Σκύλος
Cat	Γάτα
Lion	Λιοντάρι
Sheep	Πρόβατο
Pig	Χοίρος
Monkey	Μαιμού
Tiger	Τίγρης
Bear	Άρκτος
Horse	Άλογο
Bird	Πουλί

Write the right words down twice on the next page

Monkey	....	....
Cat	....	....
Bird	....	....
Lion	....	....
Sheep	....	....
Pig	....	....
Monkey	....	....
Tiger	....	....
Bear	....	....
Horse	....	....
Bird	....	....
Dog	....	....
Cat	....	....
Lion	....	....
Sheep	....	....
Pig	....	....
Horse	....	....
Tiger	....	....
Bear	....	....
Dog	....	....

Week 1

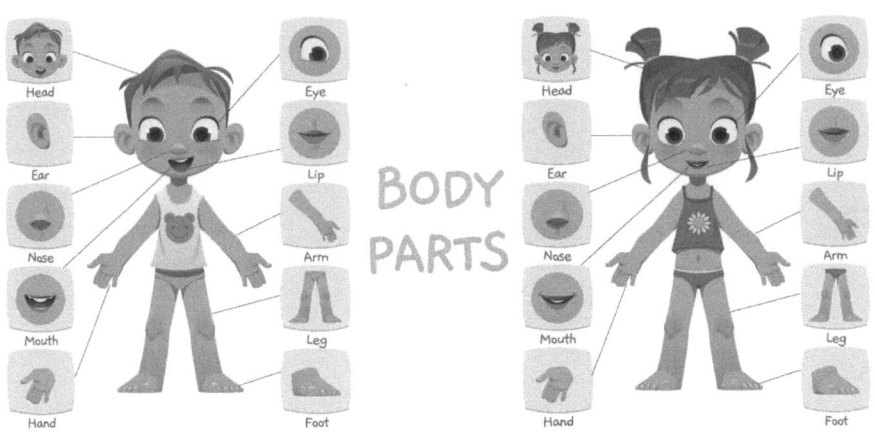

Day 6: Body

Head	Κεφάλι
Neck	Τράχηλος
Belly	Κοιλιά
Shoulder	Ώμος
Knee	Γόνατο
Back	Πλάτη
Arms	Χέρια
Hands	Χέρια
Legs	Πόδια
Feet	Πόδια

Write the right words down twice on the next page

Shoulder	....	....
Back	....	....
Feet	....	....
Belly	....	....
Hands	....	....
Shoulder	....	....
Knee	....	....
Back	....	....
Arms	....	....
Hands	....	....
Neck	....	....
Feet	....	....
Head	....	....
Neck	....	....
Belly	....	....
Knee	....	....
Legs	....	....
Arms	....	....
Head	....	....
Legs	....	....

Week 1

Day 7: Weather

Sun	Ηλιος
Rain	Βροχή
Cloud	Νέφος
Wind	Άνεμος
Snow	Χιόνι
Thunder	Κεραυνός
Lightning	Αστραπή
Storm	Καταιγίδα
Fog	Ομίχλη
Rainbow	Ουράνιο τόξο

Write the right words down twice on the next page

Storm	....	....
Rain	....	....
Fog	....	....
Snow	....	....
Cloud	....	....
Wind	....	....
Snow	....	....
Thunder	....	....
Rain	....	....
Lightning	....	....
Storm	....	....
Fog	....	....
Rainbow	....	....
Sun	....	....
Cloud	....	....
Wind	....	....
Thunder	....	....
Lightning	....	....
Rainbow	....	....
Sun	....	....

Week 2

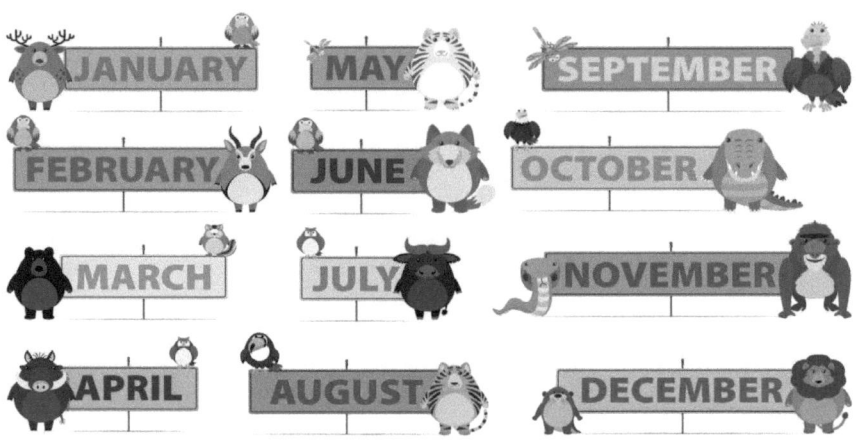

Day 8: Months

January	Ιανουάριος
February	Φεβρουάριος
March	Μάρτιος
April	Απρίλιος
May	Μάιος
June	Ιούνιος
July	Ιούλιος
August	Αύγουστος
September	Σεπτέμβριος
October	Οκτώβριος

Write the right words down twice on the next page

October	....	....
February	....	....
August	....	....
October	....	....
April	....	....
May	....	....
June	....	....
August	....	....
March	....	....
September	....	....
May	....	....
January	....	....
July	....	....
March	....	....
April	....	....
June	....	....
January	....	....
July	....	....
February	....	....
September	....	....

Week 2

Day 9: School

Teacher	Καθηγητής
Student	Μαθητής
Classroom	Αίθουσα μαθημάτων
Book	Βιβλίο
Pen	Στυλό
Pencil	Μολύβι
Desk	Γραφείο
Chair	Καρέκλα
Homework	Ασκήσεις
Exam	Εξέταση

Write the right words down twice on the next page

Chair	....	....
Homework	....	....
Teacher	....	....
Student	....	....
Classroom	....	....
Exam	....	....
Pen	....	....
Pencil	....	....
Desk	....	....
Classroom	....	....
Homework	....	....
Exam	....	....
Teacher	....	....
Student	....	....
Desk	....	....
Book	....	....
Pen	....	....
Pencil	....	....
Chair	....	....
Book	....	....

Week 2

Day 10: Transportation

Car	Αυτοκίνητο
Bus	Λεωφορείο
Train	Τρένο
Bicycle	Ποδήλατο
Motorcycle	Μοτοσυκλέτα
Boat	Σκάφος
Airplane	Αεροπλάνο
Helicopter	Ελικόπτερο
Truck	Φορτηγό
Metro	Μετρό

Write the right words down twice on the next page

Airplane	....	....
Bus	....	....
Train	....	....
Metro	....	....
Truck	....	....
Motorcycle	....	....
Boat	....	....
Airplane	....	....
Helicopter	....	....
Truck	....	....
Metro	....	....
Car	....	....
Bus	....	....
Train	....	....
Bicycle	....	....
Helicopter	....	....
Motorcycle	....	....
Boat	....	....
Bicycle	....	....
Car	....	....

Week 2

Day 11: Clothing

Shirt	Πουκάμισο
Pants	Παντελόνια
Dress	Φόρεμα
Skirt	Φούστα
Jacket	Μπουφάν
Shoes	Παπούτσια
Socks	Κάλτσες
Hat	Καπέλο
Gloves	Γάντια
Scarf	Κασκόλ

Write the right words down twice on the next page

Socks	....	....
Pants	....	....
Dress	....	....
Jacket	....	....
Skirt	....	....
Scarf	....	....
Shoes	....	....
Socks	....	....
Hat	....	....
Gloves	....	....
Scarf	....	....
Shirt	....	....
Pants	....	....
Dress	....	....
Skirt	....	....
Jacket	....	....
Shoes	....	....
Gloves	....	....
Hat	....	....
Shirt	....	....

Week 2

Day 12: Emotions

Happy	Χαρούμενος
Sad	Λυπημένος
Angry	Θυμωμένος
Excited	Ενθουσιασμένος
Surprised	Εκπληκτος
Scared	Τρομαγμένος
Nervous	Νευριασμένος
Bored	Βαρεμένος
Confused	Συγχυσμένος
Calm	Ήρεμος

Write the right words down twice on the next page

Confused	....	....
Happy	....	....
Calm	....	....
Surprised	....	....
Sad	....	....
Angry	....	....
Excited	....	....
Nervous	....	....
Scared	....	....
Nervous	....	....
Bored	....	....
Scared	....	....
Calm	....	....
Happy	....	....
Sad	....	....
Bored	....	....
Angry	....	....
Excited	....	....
Surprised	....	....
Confused	....	....

Week 2

Day 13: Hobbies

Reading	Ανάγνωση
Painting	Ζωγραφική
Singing	Τραγούδι
Dancing	Χορός
Cooking	Μαγείρεμα
Photography	Φωτογραφία
Sleeping	Ύπνος
Writing	Γραφή
Gardening	Κήπος
Sports	Αθλήματα

Write the right words down twice on the next page

Gardening	....	....
Painting	....	....
Photography	....	....
Painting	....	....
Dancing	....	....
Cooking	....	....
Photography	....	....
Sports	....	....
Writing	....	....
Gardening	....	....
Sports	....	....
Reading	....	....
Sleeping	....	....
Singing	....	....
Dancing	....	....
Cooking	....	....
Singing	....	....
Sleeping	....	....
Writing	....	....
Reading	....	....

Week 2

Day 14: Sports

Football	Ποδόσφαιρο
Basketball	Μπάσκετ
Tennis	Τένις
Swimming	Κολύμβηση
Volleyball	Βόλεϊ
Golf	Γκολφ
Cycling	Ποδηλασία
Running	Τρέξιμο
Fitness	Φυσική κατάσταση
Martial arts	Πολεμικές τέχνες

Write the right words down twice on the next page

Swimming	....	....
Football	....	....
Fitness	....	....
Basketball	....	....
Golf	....	....
Swimming	....	....
Volleyball	....	....
Golf	....	....
Running	....	....
Cycling	....	....
Running	....	....
Fitness	....	....
Martial arts	....	....
Football	....	....
Basketball	....	....
Tennis	....	....
Martial arts	....	....
Volleyball	....	....
Cycling	....	....
Tennis	....	....

Week 3

Day 15: Nature

Tree	Δέντρο
Flower	Λουλούδι
River	Ποτάμι
Mountain	Βουνό
Lake	Λίμνη
Beach	Παραλία
Forest	Δάσος
Grass	Γρασίδι
Star	Αστέρι
Cloud	Νέφος

Write the right words down twice on the next page

Grass	....	....
Beach	....	....
Mountain	....	....
Cloud	....	....
Flower	....	....
River	....	....
Mountain	....	....
Lake	....	....
Beach	....	....
Forest	....	....
Grass	....	....
Star	....	....
Forest	....	....
Cloud	....	....
Tree	....	....
Flower	....	....
River	....	....
Star	....	....
Lake	....	....
Tree	....	....

Week 3

Day 16: Days of the Week

Monday	Δευτέρα
Tuesday	Τρίτη
Wednesday	Τετάρτη
Thursday	Πέμπτη
Friday	Παρασκευή
Saturday	Σάββατο
Sunday	Κυριακή
Yesterday	Χθες
Tomorrow	Αύριο
Today	Σήμερα

Write the right words down twice on the next page

Sunday	....	....
Tuesday	....	....
Saturday	....	....
Today	....	....
Wednesday	....	....
Tomorrow	....	....
Friday	....	....
Saturday	....	....
Yesterday	....	....
Tomorrow	....	....
Today	....	....
Monday	....	....
Thursday	....	....
Wednesday	....	....
Thursday	....	....
Friday	....	....
Monday	....	....
Sunday	....	....
Yesterday	....	....
Tuesday	....	....

Week 3

Day 17: Music

Song	Τραγούδι
Melody	Μελωδία
Rhythm	Ρυθμός
Instrument	Όργανο
Singing	Τραγούδι
Band	Συγκρότημα
Concert	Συναυλία
Piano	Πιάνο
Guitar	Κιθάρα
Sound	Ήχος

Write the right words down twice on the next page

Concert ....

Melody ....

Rhythm ....

Sound ....

Guitar ....

Piano ....

Instrument ....

Singing ....

Band ....

Piano ....

Guitar ....

Sound ....

Song ....

Rhythm ....

Instrument ....

Singing ....

Band ....

Concert ....

Song ....

Melody ....

Week 3

Day 18: Jobs

Teacher	Δάσκαλος
Doctor	Γιατρός
Engineer	Μηχανικός
Chef	Σεφ
Police officer	Αστυνομικός
Firefighter	Πυροσβέστης
Nurse	Νοσοκόμα
Pilot	Πιλότος
Lawyer	Δικηγόρος
Artist	Καλλιτέχνης

Write the right words down twice on the next page

Lawyer	....	....
Teacher	....	....
Chef	....	....
Doctor	....	....
Engineer	....	....
Chef	....	....
Police officer	....	....
Pilot	....	....
Nurse	....	....
Doctor	....	....
Artist	....	....
Teacher	....	....
Pilot	....	....
Engineer	....	....
Artist	....	....
Police officer	....	....
Firefighter	....	....
Nurse	....	....
Lawyer	....	....
Firefighter	....	....

Week 3

Day 19: Fruits

Apple	Μήλο
Banana	Μπανάνα
Orange	Πορτοκάλι
Strawberry	Φράουλα
Grapes	Σταφύλια
Watermelon	Καρπούζι
Pineapple	Ανανάς
Mango	Μάνγκο
Kiwi	Κίουι
Peach	Ροδάκινο

Write the right words down twice on the next page

Orange	....	....
Apple	....	....
Banana	....	....
Orange	....	....
Mango	....	....
Grapes	....	....
Kiwi	....	....
Pineapple	....	....
Mango	....	....
Peach	....	....
Apple	....	....
Banana	....	....
Strawberry	....	....
Grapes	....	....
Watermelon	....	....
Pineapple	....	....
Kiwi	....	....
Strawberry	....	....
Peach	....	....
Watermelon	....	....

Week 3

Day 20: Vegetables

Carrot	Καρότο
Tomato	Ντομάτα
Potato	Πατάτα
Onion	Κρεμμύδι
Cucumber	Αγγούρι
Broccoli	Μπρόκολο
Spinach	Σπανάκι
Corn	Καλαμπόκι
Cabbage	Λάχανο
Mushroom	Μανιτάρι

Write the right words down twice on the next page

Corn	....	....
Tomato	....	....
Potato	....	....
Mushroom	....	....
Spinach	....	....
Onion	....	....
Broccoli	....	....
Spinach	....	....
Corn	....	....
Tomato	....	....
Mushroom	....	....
Carrot	....	....
Cucumber	....	....
Potato	....	....
Onion	....	....
Cucumber	....	....
Cabbage	....	....
Carrot	....	....
Cabbage	....	....
Broccoli	....	....

Week 3

Day 21: Tools

Hammer	Σφυρί
Screwdriver	Κατσαβίδι
Wrench	Ροδέλα
Pliers	Σφιγκτήρας
Saw	Πριόνι
Drill	Τρυπάνι
Tape measure	Μέτρο
Chisel	Σφιγκτήρας
Level	Σκαπάνη
Paintbrush	Πινέλο

Write the right words down twice on the next page

Level	....	....
Screwdriver	....	....
Wrench	....	....
Paintbrush	....	....
Pliers	....	....
Drill	....	....
Chisel	....	....
Level	....	....
Paintbrush	....	....
Hammer	....	....
Screwdriver	....	....
Pliers	....	....
Saw	....	....
Drill	....	....
Tape measure	....	....
Hammer	....	....
Wrench	....	....
Saw	....	....
Chisel	....	....
Tape measure	....	....

Week 4

Day 22: Kitchen

Plate	Πιάτο
Fork	Πιρούνι
Knife	Μαχαίρι
Spoon	Κουτάλι
Cup	Κούπα
Bowl	Μπολ
Pan	Τηγάνι
Pot	Κατσαρόλα
Cutting board	Σανίδα κοπής
Oven	Φούρνος

Write the right words down twice on the next page

Plate	....	....
Oven	....	....
Fork	....	....
Bowl	....	....
Knife	....	....
Spoon	....	....
Cup	....	....
Cutting board	....	....
Knife	....	....
Fork	....	....
Bowl	....	....
Spoon	....	....
Pan	....	....
Pot	....	....
Cutting board	....	....
Oven	....	....
Pot	....	....
Plate	....	....
Cup	....	....
Pan	....	....

Week 4

Day 23: Instruments

Guitar	Κιθάρα
Piano	Πιάνο
Violin	Βιολί
Flute	Φλογέρα
Trumpet	Τρομπέτα
Drum	Ντραμς
Saxophone	Σαξόφωνο
Cello	Τσέλο
Clarinet	Κλαρινέτο
Harp	Άρπα

Write the right words down twice on the next page

Flute	....	....
Piano	....	....
Trumpet	....	....
Violin	....	....
Cello	....	....
Trumpet	....	....
Drum	....	....
Saxophone	....	....
Cello	....	....
Clarinet	....	....
Violin	....	....
Saxophone	....	....
Harp	....	....
Guitar	....	....
Drum	....	....
Piano	....	....
Harp	....	....
Flute	....	....
Guitar	....	....
Clarinet	....	....

Week 4

Day 24: Buildings

House	Σπίτι
School	Σχολείο
Hospital	Νοσοκομείο
Library	Βιβλιοθήκη
Bank	Τράπεζα
Restaurant	Εστιατόριο
Hotel	Ξενοδοχείο
Museum	Μουσείο
Church	Εκκλησία
Stadium	Στάδιο

Write the right words down twice on the next page

Hospital	....	....
House	....	....
Museum	....	....
School	....	....
Stadium	....	....
Hospital	....	....
Church	....	....
Restaurant	....	....
Hotel	....	....
Museum	....	....
Church	....	....
House	....	....
School	....	....
Library	....	....
Bank	....	....
Restaurant	....	....
Hotel	....	....
Library	....	....
Bank	....	....
Stadium	....	....

Week 4

Day 25: Directions

Left	Αριστερά
Right	Δεξιά
Straight	Ευθεία
Up	Πάνω
Down	Κάτω
North	Βόρεια
South	Νότια
East	Ανατολικά
West	Δυτικά
Stop	Σταμάτα

Write the right words down twice on the next page

Straight	....	....
Left	....	....
South	....	....
Straight	....	....
Up	....	....
Down	....	....
North	....	....
Stop	....	....
East	....	....
Stop	....	....
Left	....	....
Right	....	....
South	....	....
Right	....	....
North	....	....
West	....	....
Up	....	....
Down	....	....
East	....	....
West	....	....

Week 4

Day 26: Bedroom

Bed	Κρεβάτι
Pillow	Μαξιλάρι
Blanket	Κουβέρτα
Wardrobe	Ντουλάπα
Nightstand	Κομοδίνο
Lamp	Λάμπα
Alarm clock	Ξυπνητήρι
Dresser	Συρταριέρα
Hanger	Κρεμάστρα
Mirror	Καθρέπτης

Write the right words down twice on the next page

Hanger	....	....
Pillow	....	....
Dresser	....	....
Wardrobe	....	....
Mirror	....	....
Nightstand	....	....
Lamp	....	....
Alarm clock	....	....
Dresser	....	....
Blanket	....	....
Hanger	....	....
Mirror	....	....
Wardrobe	....	....
Nightstand	....	....
Bed	....	....
Blanket	....	....
Lamp	....	....
Bed	....	....
Alarm clock	....	....
Pillow	....	....

Week 4

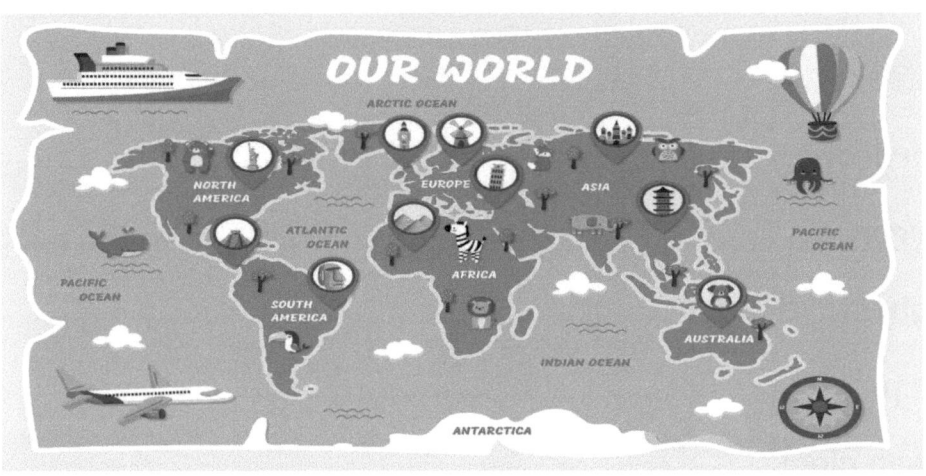

Day 27: Countries

United States	Ηνωμένες Πολιτείες
United Kingdom	Ηνωμένο Βασίλειο
Canada	Καναδάς
Australia	Αυστραλία
Germany	Γερμανία
France	Γαλλία
China	Κίνα
Japan	Ιαπωνία
Brazil	Βραζιλία
India	Ινδία

Write the right words down twice on the next page

China ....

United States ....

India ....

Canada ....

Australia ....

Brazil ....

China ....

Japan ....

Brazil ....

India ....

United States ....

Germany ....

Canada ....

Australia ....

Japan ....

United Kingdom ....

Germany ....

France ....

United Kingdom ....

France ....

Week 4

Day 28: Travel

Airport	Αεροδρόμιο
Passport	Διαβατήριο
Ticket	Εισιτήριο
Suitcase	Βαλίτσα
Hotel	Ξενοδοχείο
Sightseeing	Αξιοθέατα
Beach	Παραλία
Adventure	Περιπέτεια
Map	Χάρτης
Tourist	Τουρίστας

Write the right words down twice on the next page

Airport	....	....
Adventure	....	....
Passport	....	....
Ticket	....	....
Suitcase	....	....
Hotel	....	....
Sightseeing	....	....
Beach	....	....
Adventure	....	....
Map	....	....
Tourist	....	....
Airport	....	....
Passport	....	....
Ticket	....	....
Suitcase	....	....
Hotel	....	....
Sightseeing	....	....
Beach	....	....
Map	....	....
Tourist	....	....

Week 5

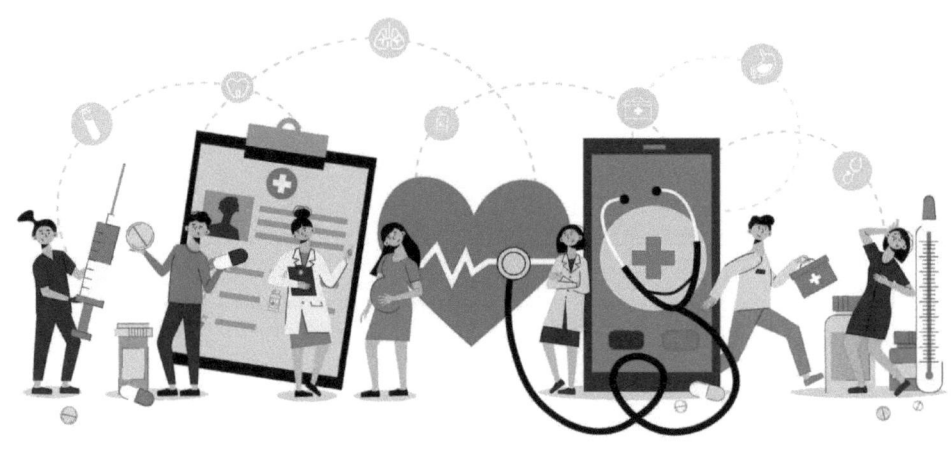

Day 29: Health

Doctor	Γιατρός
Hospital	Νοσοκομείο
Medicine	Φάρμακο
Nurse	Νοσοκόμα
Pain	Πόνος
Appointment	Ραντεβού
Exercise	Άσκηση
Sleep	Ύπνος
Diet	Δίαιτα
Vitamin	Βιταμίνη

Write the right words down twice on the next page

Appointment	....	....
Vitamin	....	....
Hospital	....	....
Medicine	....	....
Nurse	....	....
Pain	....	....
Sleep	....	....
Hospital	....	....
Exercise	....	....
Nurse	....	....
Sleep	....	....
Diet	....	....
Vitamin	....	....
Doctor	....	....
Pain	....	....
Appointment	....	....
Exercise	....	....
Doctor	....	....
Medicine	....	....
Diet	....	....

Week 5

Day 30: Languages

English	Αγγλικά
Spanish	Ισπανικά
Greek	Γαλλικά
German	Γερμανικά
Dutch	Ολλανδικά
Frisian	Φριζιανά
Russian	Ρωσικά
Portuguese	Πορτογαλικά
Japanese	Ιαπωνικά
Italian	Ιταλικά

Write the right words down twice on the next page

German	....	....
Spanish	....	....
Portuguese	....	....
Greek	....	....
German	....	....
Dutch	....	....
Frisian	....	....
Russian	....	....
Italian	....	....
Russian	....	....
Japanese	....	....
Frisian	....	....
English	....	....
Italian	....	....
English	....	....
Spanish	....	....
Greek	....	....
Dutch	....	....
Portuguese	....	....
Japanese	....	....

Week 5

Day 31: Church

Priest	Ιερέας
Worship	Λατρεία
Prayer	Προσευχή
Bible	Βίβλος
Sermon	Ομιλία
Choir	Χορωδία
Altar	Θυσιαστήριο
Cross	Σταυρός
Faith	Πίστη
Ceremony	Τελετή

Write the right words down twice on the next page

Choir	....	....
Worship	....	....
Altar	....	....
Bible	....	....
Ceremony	....	....
Faith	....	....
Sermon	....	....
Choir	....	....
Altar	....	....
Cross	....	....
Faith	....	....
Ceremony	....	....
Cross	....	....
Priest	....	....
Worship	....	....
Prayer	....	....
Bible	....	....
Sermon	....	....
Priest	....	....
Prayer	....	....

Week 5

Day 32: Birds

Eagle	Αετός
Sparrow	Σπουργίτης
Owl	Κουκουβάγια
Parrot	Παπαγάλος
Hummingbird	Κολιμπρί
Pigeon	Περιστέρι
Flamingo	Φλαμίνγκο
Swan	Κύκνος
Peacock	Ταύρος
Duck	Πάπια

Write the right words down twice on the next page

Duck	....	....
Eagle	....	....
Sparrow	....	....
Owl	....	....
Eagle	....	....
Swan	....	....
Sparrow	....	....
Flamingo	....	....
Hummingbird	....	....
Pigeon	....	....
Flamingo	....	....
Owl	....	....
Swan	....	....
Peacock	....	....
Duck	....	....
Parrot	....	....
Hummingbird	....	....
Pigeon	....	....
Parrot	....	....
Peacock	....	....

Week 5

Day 33: Science

Chemistry	Χημεία
Biology	Βιολογία
Physics	Φυσική
Astronomy	Αστρονομία
Experiment	Πείραμα
Laboratory	Εργαστήριο
Microscope	Μικροσκόπιο
Hypothesis	Υπόθεση
Scientist	Επιστήμητής
Discovery	Ανακάλυψη

Write the right words down twice on the next page

Hypothesis	....	....
Biology	....	....
Experiment	....	....
Astronomy	....	....
Physics	....	....
Astronomy	....	....
Microscope	....	....
Scientist	....	....
Laboratory	....	....
Physics	....	....
Microscope	....	....
Hypothesis	....	....
Chemistry	....	....
Scientist	....	....
Discovery	....	....
Chemistry	....	....
Biology	....	....
Laboratory	....	....
Discovery	....	....
Experiment	....	....

Week 5

Day 34: Film

Actor	Ηθοποιός
Actress	Ηθοποιός
Director	Σκηνοθέτης
Script	Σενάριο
Camera	Κάμερα
Scene	Σκηνή
Drama	Δράμα
Comedy	Κωμωδία
Action	Δράση
Television	Τηλεόραση

Write the right words down twice on the next page

Actor	....	....
Camera	....	....
Action	....	....
Director	....	....
Script	....	....
Television	....	....
Camera	....	....
Scene	....	....
Drama	....	....
Comedy	....	....
Action	....	....
Television	....	....
Actor	....	....
Actress	....	....
Director	....	....
Scene	....	....
Actress	....	....
Drama	....	....
Comedy	....	....
Script	....	....

Week 5

Day 35: History

Ancient	Αρχαίος
Civilization	Πολιτισμός
Emperor	Αυτοκράτορας
Revolution	Επανάσταση
War	Πόλεμος
Kingdom	Βασίλειο
Archaeology	Αρχαιολογία
Renaissance	Αναγέννηση
Independence	Ανεξαρτησία
Event	Εκδήλωση

Write the right words down twice on the next page

Kingdom	....	....
Event	....	....
Archaeology	....	....
Emperor	....	....
Renaissance	....	....
Independence	....	....
Revolution	....	....
War	....	....
Kingdom	....	....
Archaeology	....	....
Renaissance	....	....
Independence	....	....
Event	....	....
Ancient	....	....
Civilization	....	....
Emperor	....	....
Revolution	....	....
War	....	....
Ancient	....	....
Civilization	....	....

Week 6

Day 36: Drinks

Water	Νερό
Coffee	Καφές
Tea	Τσάι
Juice	Χυμός
Soda	Αναψυκτικό
Milk	Γάλα
Wine	Κρασί
Beer	Μπύρα
Cocktail	Κοκτέιλ
Lemonade	Λεμονάδα

Write the right words down twice on the next page

Soda	....	....
Cocktail	....	....
Tea	....	....
Juice	....	....
Wine	....	....
Soda	....	....
Milk	....	....
Wine	....	....
Beer	....	....
Cocktail	....	....
Lemonade	....	....
Water	....	....
Coffee	....	....
Water	....	....
Tea	....	....
Lemonade	....	....
Juice	....	....
Milk	....	....
Coffee	....	....
Beer	....	....

Week 6

Day 37: Business

Entrepreneur	Επιχειρηματίας
Company	Εταιρεία
Marketing	Μάρκετινγκ
Sales	Πωλήσεις
Product	Προϊόν
Customer	Πελάτης
Finance	Οικονομικά
Strategy	Στρατηγική
Profit	Κέρδος
Investment	Επένδυση

Write the right words down twice on the next page

Strategy	....	....
Company	....	....
Marketing	....	....
Sales	....	....
Product	....	....
Customer	....	....
Finance	....	....
Investment	....	....
Customer	....	....
Profit	....	....
Finance	....	....
Investment	....	....
Entrepreneur	....	....
Company	....	....
Marketing	....	....
Sales	....	....
Product	....	....
Profit	....	....
Entrepreneur	....	....
Strategy	....	....

Week 6

Day 38: Beach

Sand	Άμμος
Waves	Κύματα
Sunscreen	Αντηλιακό
Swim	Κολύμπι
Seashells	Κοχύλια
Umbrella	Ομπρέλα
Beach ball	Μπάλα παραλίας
Sunbathing	Ηλιοθεραπεία
Surfing	Κύματα
Picnic	Πικνίκ

Write the right words down twice on the next page

Beach ball	....	....
Sunbathing	....	....
Waves	....	....
Sunscreen	....	....
Picnic	....	....
Swim	....	....
Umbrella	....	....
Beach ball	....	....
Picnic	....	....
Sand	....	....
Sunscreen	....	....
Swim	....	....
Seashells	....	....
Surfing	....	....
Waves	....	....
Umbrella	....	....
Seashells	....	....
Sunbathing	....	....
Surfing	....	....
Sand	....	....

Week 6

Day 39: Hospital

Doctor	Γιατρός
Nurse	Νοσοκόμα
Patient	Ασθενής
Emergency	Έκτακτη ανάγκη
Surgery	Χειρουργείο
Appointment	Ραντεβού
Stethoscope	Στηθοσκόπιο
X-ray	Ακτινογραφία
Medicine	Φάρμακο
Recovery	Ανάρρωση

Write the right words down twice on the next page

Nurse ....

Doctor ....

Appointment ....

Stethoscope ....

Emergency ....

Recovery ....

Nurse ....

Patient ....

Emergency ....

Surgery ....

Appointment ....

Stethoscope ....

X-ray ....

Medicine ....

Recovery ....

Doctor ....

Surgery ....

Patient ....

X-ray ....

Medicine ....

Week 6

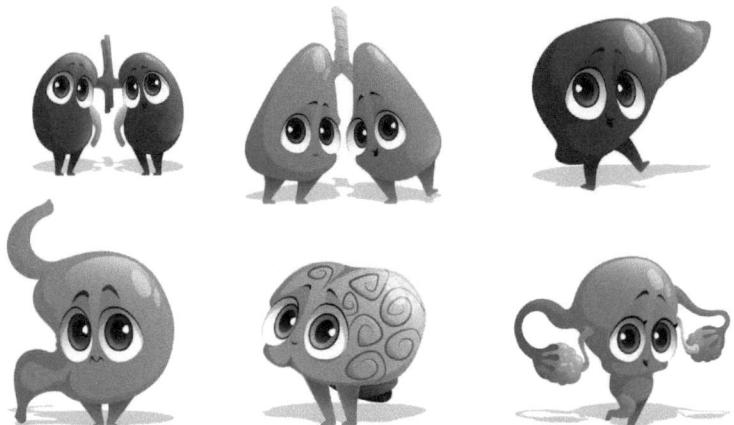

Day 40: Internal Body

Heart	Καρδιά
Lungs	Πνεύμονες
Stomach	Στομάχι
Liver	Ήπαρ
Kidneys	Νεφροί
Brain	Εγκέφαλος
Intestines	Έντερα
Bladder	Ουροδόχος κύστη
Bones	Οστά
Muscles	Μύες

Write the right words down twice on the next page

Kidneys ....

Stomach ....

Heart ....

Intestines ....

Brain ....

Lungs ....

Stomach ....

Liver ....

Muscles ....

Kidneys ....

Intestines ....

Bladder ....

Bones ....

Muscles ....

Heart ....

Lungs ....

Bones ....

Liver ....

Brain ....

Bladder ....

Week 6

Day 41: Internet

Website	Ιστοσελίδα
Email	Ηλεκτρονικό ταχυδρομείο
Social media	Κοινωνικά μέσα ενημέρωσης
Online shopping	Αγορές μέσω διαδικτύου
Search engine	Μηχανή αναζήτησης
Password	Κωδικός πρόσβασης
Wi-Fi	Ασύρματο δίκτυο
Download	Λήψη
Upload	Μεταφόρτωση
Browser	Πρόγραμμα περιήγησης

Write the right words down twice on the next page

Browser	....	....
Website	....	....
Email	....	....
Social media	....	....
Wi-Fi	....	....
Search engine	....	....
Password	....	....
Wi-Fi	....	....
Download	....	....
Upload	....	....
Browser	....	....
Online shopping	....	....
Email	....	....
Social media	....	....
Online shopping	....	....
Password	....	....
Website	....	....
Download	....	....
Upload	....	....
Search engine	....	....

Week 6

Day 42: Shapes

Cirkel	Κύκλος
Square	Τετράγωνο
Rectangle	Ορθογώνιο
Triangle	Τρίγωνο
Oval	Οβάλ
Pyramid	Πυραμίδα
Cube	Κύβος
Arrow	Βέλος
Star	Αστέρι
Cylinder	Κύλινδρος

Write the right words down twice on the next page

Rectangle	....	....
Triangle	....	....
Pyramid	....	....
Arrow	....	....
Star	....	....
Cylinder	....	....
Oval	....	....
Square	....	....
Star	....	....
Cube	....	....
Cirkel	....	....
Pyramid	....	....
Cylinder	....	....
Cirkel	....	....
Square	....	....
Rectangle	....	....
Triangle	....	....
Oval	....	....
Cube	....	....
Arrow	....	....

Week 7

Day 43: House Parts

Roof	Στέγη
Door	Πόρτα
Window	Παράθυρο
Floor	Δάπεδο
Wall	Τοίχος
Ceiling	Οροφή
Stairs	Σκάλες
Bathroom	Μπάνιο
Kitchen	Κουζίνα
Bedroom	Κρεβατοκάμαρα

Write the right words down twice on the next page

Wall ....

Door ....

Stairs ....

Ceiling ....

Floor ....

Wall ....

Ceiling ....

Bedroom ....

Stairs ....

Bathroom ....

Kitchen ....

Bedroom ....

Roof ....

Door ....

Window ....

Floor ....

Roof ....

Bathroom ....

Kitchen ....

Window ....

Week 7

Day 44: Around the House

Plant	Φυτό
Watering can	Κανάτα ποτίσματος
Shed	Αποθήκη
Doorbell	Κουδούνι
Fence	Φράχτης
Mailbox	Ταχυδρομικό κουτί
Lawn mower	Γκαζονοκοπτική μηχανή
Wheelbarrow	Τροχοφόρο
Shovel	Σκαπτικό
Bench	Παγκάκι

Write the right words down twice on the next page

Watering can	....	....
Shed	....	....
Doorbell	....	....
Mailbox	....	....
Bench	....	....
Fence	....	....
Wheelbarrow	....	....
Shed	....	....
Mailbox	....	....
Bench	....	....
Lawn mower	....	....
Wheelbarrow	....	....
Shovel	....	....
Plant	....	....
Watering can	....	....
Doorbell	....	....
Fence	....	....
Lawn mower	....	....
Shovel	....	....
Plant	....	....

Week 7

Day 45: Face

Eyes	Μάτια
Nose	Μύτη
Mouth	Στόμα
Ears	Αυτιά
Cheeks	Μάγουλα
Forehead	Μέτωπο
Chin	Πηγούνι
Lips	Χείλη
Teeth	Δόντια
Eyebrows	Φρύδια

Write the right words down twice on the next page

Eyebrows ....

Nose ....

Chin ....

Forehead ....

Ears ....

Cheeks ....

Forehead ....

Chin ....

Nose ....

Lips ....

Teeth ....

Eyebrows ....

Eyes ....

Lips ....

Teeth ....

Mouth ....

Ears ....

Mouth ....

Cheeks ....

Eyes ....

Week 7

Day 46: Bathroom

Sink	Νιπτήρας
Toilet	Τουαλέτα
Shower	Ντους
Bathtub	Μπανιέρα
Mirror	Καθρέφτης
Towel	Πετσέτα
Soap	Σαπούνι
Toothbrush	Οδοντόβουρτσα
Shampoo	Σαμπουάν
Hairdryer	Σεσουάρ

Write the right words down twice on the next page

Mirror	....	....
Sink	....	....
Hairdryer	....	....
Shower	....	....
Bathtub	....	....
Mirror	....	....
Towel	....	....
Soap	....	....
Toothbrush	....	....
Toilet	....	....
Shampoo	....	....
Towel	....	....
Soap	....	....
Hairdryer	....	....
Sink	....	....
Toilet	....	....
Shower	....	....
Bathtub	....	....
Toothbrush	....	....
Shampoo	....	....

Week 7

Day 47: Living Room

Sofa	Καναπές
Television	Τηλεόραση
Coffee table	Τραπεζάκι σαλονιού
Bookshelf	Βιβλιοθήκη
Lamp	Λάμπα
Rug	Χαλί
Cushion	Μαξιλάρι
Remote control	Τηλεχειριστήριο
Curtains	Κουρτίνες
Fireplace	Τζάκι

Write the right words down twice on the next page

Rug	....	....
Sofa	....	....
Remote control	....	....
Television	....	....
Coffee table	....	....
Bookshelf	....	....
Lamp	....	....
Cushion	....	....
Curtains	....	....
Fireplace	....	....
Sofa	....	....
Television	....	....
Fireplace	....	....
Lamp	....	....
Rug	....	....
Cushion	....	....
Remote control	....	....
Curtains	....	....
Bookshelf	....	....
Coffee table	....	....

Week 7

Day 48: Finance

Budget	Προϋπολογισμός
Savings	Αποταμίευση
Debt	Χρέος
Income	Εισόδημα
Expenses	Έξοδα
Bank account	Τραπεζικός λογαριασμός
Credit card	Πιστωτική κάρτα
Interest	Επιτόκιο
Loan	Δάνειο
Stock market	Χρηματιστήριο

Write the right words down twice on the next page

Savings	....	....
Loan	....	....
Debt	....	....
Income	....	....
Expenses	....	....
Budget	....	....
Income	....	....
Expenses	....	....
Interest	....	....
Loan	....	....
Stock market	....	....
Budget	....	....
Bank account	....	....
Credit card	....	....
Debt	....	....
Savings	....	....
Interest	....	....
Bank account	....	....
Credit card	....	....
Stock market	....	....

Week 7

Day 49: Books

Writer	Συγγραφέας
Page	Σελίδα
Table of Contents	Πίνακας περιεχομένων
Foreword	Πρόλογος
Introduction	Εισαγωγή
Front cover	Εξώφυλλο
Back cover	Οπισθόφυλλο
Text	Κείμενο
Title	Τίτλος
Picture	Εικόνα

Write the right words down twice on the next page

Front cover ....

Table of Contents ....

Title ....

Picture ....

Introduction ....

Back cover ....

Page ....

Foreword ....

Title ....

Text ....

Back cover ....

Picture ....

Writer ....

Page ....

Table of Contents ....

Foreword ....

Introduction ....

Front cover ....

Writer ....

Text ....

Week 8

Day 50: Law

Witness	Μάρτυρας
Justice	Δικαιοσύνη
Judge	Δικαστής
Victim	Θύμα
Perpetrator	Υπαίτιος
Court	Δικαστήριο
Evidence	Αποδείξεις
Lawyer	Δικηγόρος
Crime	Έγκλημα
Government	Κυβέρνηση

Write the right words down twice on the next page

Perpetrator ....

Court ....

Justice ....

Evidence ....

Victim ....

Government ....

Judge ....

Victim ....

Perpetrator ....

Court ....

Evidence ....

Lawyer ....

Crime ....

Government ....

Witness ....

Justice ....

Crime ....

Judge ....

Witness ....

Lawyer ....

Help Us Share Your Thoughts!

Dear Reader,

Thank you for choosing to read our book. We hope you enjoyed the journey through its pages and that it left a positive impact on your life. As an independent author, reviews from readers like you are incredibly valuable in helping us reach a wider audience and improve our craft.

If you enjoyed our book, we kindly ask for a moment of your time to leave an honest review. Your feedback can make a world of difference by providing potential readers with insight into the book's content and your personal experience.

Your review doesn't have to be lengthy or complicated—just a few lines expressing your genuine thoughts would be immensely appreciated. We value your feedback and take it to heart, using it to shape our future work and create more content that resonates with readers like you.

By leaving a review, you are not only supporting us as authors but also helping other readers discover this book. Your voice matters, and your words have the power to inspire others to embark on this literary journey.

We genuinely appreciate your time and willingness to share your thoughts. Thank you for being an essential part of our author journey.